She was a queen who wore her pain like a crown.
She gathered her strength from the storm."

— Rupi Kaur

My Inner Queen Has Come Forth

AARON L. HOUSTON

To the Queen in Every Woman,

This book is dedicated to you—bold, resilient, and radiant daughters of the King. It is dedicated to the dreamers, nurturers, warriors, and seekers of truth who dare to believe in their worth, their power, and their purpose.

To the mothers, daughters, sisters, and friends who understand the depth of their value, the beauty of their uniqueness, and the strength of their resilience.

May the words within these pages ignite a fire within you—a fire to reclaim your throne, embrace your sovereignty, and walk in the fullness of your identity as daughters of the Most High God.

May you find inspiration, encouragement, and empowerment to break free from the chains of self-doubt, societal expectations, and past hurts and step into the fullness of your calling as queens in God's kingdom.

This book is dedicated to you, dear reader, with the utmost respect and admiration for the incredible journey that lies ahead.

Here is to your growth, your maturity, and your unapologetic embrace of the queen that God has destined you to be.

With deep appreciation and anticipation for the journey ahead.

Aaron L. Houston

TABLE OF CONTENTS

Dear Reader,

Welcome to this amazing journey of empowerment, discovery, and transformation. As you hold this book in your hands, know that you are journeying on a path that has the potential to revolutionize your perspective, ignite your passion, and unleash your inner queen.

In these pages, I share insights, reflections, and practical wisdom gathered from my own journey as a husband, leader, brother, and father—a journey marked by challenges, triumphs, and moments of profound revelation. Through it all, I have come to understand the unique calling and incredible potential that each woman possesses.

This book is not just a collection of words; it is a manifesto—a call to arms for women everywhere to rise up, stand tall, and reclaim their rightful place as queens in God's kingdom. It is a reminder that you are fearfully and wonderfully made, endowed with gifts, talents, and a destiny that only you can fulfill.

Within these chapters, you will find stories of courage, lessons in resilience, and principles for living a life of purpose, passion, and power. Whether you are navigating the intricacies of relationships, pursuing your dreams and aspirations, or overcoming obstacles that stand in your way, I hope that you will find something here that profoundly resonates with you— that overwhelmingly inspires you to embrace your worth, celebrate your uniqueness, and walk boldly in the fullness of who God created you to be.

As you read these words, I encourage you to approach them with an open heart and a receptive spirit. Allow yourself to be challenged, encouraged, and transformed by the truths you encounter. And remember, you are not alone on this journey. There is a sisterhood of queens—women who have walked the path before you, women who walk alongside you, and women who will come after you—who are cheering you on, lifting you up, and celebrating your victories.

So, dear reader, I invite you to dive in, explore, and engage with the ideas presented here. May this book be a catalyst for change, a source of inspiration, and a guide for living a life of purpose, passion, and power.

With anticipation for the journey ahead.

Aaron L. Houston

INTRODUCTION

In a world that often seeks to diminish your worth, silence your voice, and confine you to narrow definitions of beauty and success, it is time to rise up and reclaim your throne. It is time to embrace the truth of who you are—a queen, fearfully and wonderfully made, destined for greatness and called to reign with grace, dignity, and power.

Welcome to this journey of self-discovery, empowerment, and transformation. As you journey through these pages, know that you are not alone. You are part of a sisterhood—a lineage of queens who have walked the earth before you, who walk alongside you, and who will come after you. Together, you all are stronger, wiser, and more powerful than you could ever be alone.

In this book, we will explore what it means to embody the essence of royalty—to walk with confidence, speak with authority, and rule with compassion. We will delve into topics ranging from self-love and confidence to purpose and destiny, uncovering the keys to unlocking your full potential and stepping into the fullness of your calling.

But more than just a guidebook or a self-help book, this is an invitation—a call to arms for you to rise up, stand tall, and embrace the truth of who you are. You are not just a woman;

you are a queen—a daughter of the King of kings, crowned with beauty, grace, and wisdom.

So, my lady, as you journey through these pages, I invite you to open your heart, open your mind, and open your spirit to receive the truth, wisdom, and empowerment that awaits you. May this book be a mirror, reflecting back to you the incredible beauty, strength, and potential that lies within. May it be a roadmap guiding you on the path to greatness and fulfillment, and may it be a companion walking alongside you as you embrace the fullness of who you were created to be.

With love, admiration, and anticipation for the journey ahead.

Aaron L. Houston

CHAPTER 1

RISE OF THE QUEEN WITHIN

In the quiet moments of the early morning, before the world awakens and the chaos of the day begins, there exists a sacred space where the spirit stirs and whispers truths to the soul. It is within this hallowed realm that the journey of self-discovery commences, where the seeds of greatness are planted, and the rise of the queen within begins.

My dear queens, welcome to the dawn of a new era, where you are called to embrace the divine purpose etched within the very fabric of your being. You are not merely ordinary women traversing the mundane landscape of life; you are queens adorned with crowns of grace, strength, and wisdom. It is time to awaken to the truth of who you are and the power that lies dormant within you.

As Bishop T. D. Jakes often reminds us, "You were not created to be a mere spectator in the grand theatre of existence. You were designed to take center stage, to command attention with your presence, and to leave an indelible mark on the world around you." So, rise up, my sisters, and claim your rightful place as queens in the kingdom of life.

But what does it truly mean to embody the essence of a queen? It goes beyond mere external adornments or titles of nobility; it encompasses the very core of your being—the spirit, mind, and heart. It is a journey of self-discovery, self-awareness, and self-mastery—a journey that requires courage, resilience, and unwavering faith.

In the Scripture, we find echoes of this truth, whispered through the ages to women of valor who dared to rise above their circumstances and embrace their destiny. In the book of Esther, we encounter Queen Esther, a woman of humble origins thrust into a position of influence and power for such a time as this. Despite the challenges she faced, she embraced her calling with courage and conviction, declaring, "If I perish, I perish" (Esther 4:16, KJV).

Likewise, in the Gospel of Luke, we find the story of the woman with the issue of blood—a woman who had suffered for 12 long years yet found the strength to reach out and touch the hem of Jesus' garment, believing that she would be healed. And in that moment of faith, she was made whole, her identity as a daughter of the Most High affirmed for all eternity (Luke 8:43-48, KJV).

My sisters, these biblical narratives serve as a testament to the transformative power of faith, resilience, and unwavering belief in oneself. They remind us that within each of us lies the potential to overcome adversity, transcend limitations, and become the best version of ourselves.

But the journey of self-discovery and empowerment is not without its challenges. It requires you to confront your fears, embrace your vulnerabilities, and release the shackles of self-doubt that bind you. It is a journey of inner healing and renewal—a process of shedding the layers of false identities and societal expectations to reveal the radiant queen within.

So, where do we begin this journey of transformation? It begins with a shift in mindset—a conscious decision to embrace your worthiness, celebrate your uniqueness, and cultivate a deep sense of self-love and acceptance. It requires you to silence the voices of doubt and negativity that whisper lies of inadequacy and unworthiness and, instead, listen to the still, small voice within that affirms our inherent value and worth.

I have heard and I must agree with the statement, "You cannot conquer what you are not willing to confront." So, mighty woman, I encourage you to confront your fears, your insecurities, and your doubts head-on, knowing that you do not walk this journey alone. For within each of you resides the spirit of the Most High—the same spirit that breathed life into creation, the same spirit that empowers us to rise above every obstacle and adversity.

As you embark on this sacred journey of self-discovery and empowerment, let us remember the words of the psalmist: "I will praise thee; for I am fearfully and wonderfully made:

marvelous are thy works; and that my soul knoweth right well" (Psalm 139:14, KJV). You are fearfully and wonderfully made, my sisters—never forget that.

So, rise up, queens, and embrace the divine destiny that awaits you. The world is waiting for the radiance of your presence, the brilliance of your wisdom, and the depth of your compassion. You are queens—beautiful, powerful, and destined for greatness. It is time to claim your throne and reign with grace, dignity, and strength, for the rise of the queen begins now.

CHAPTER 2

GRIT AND GRACE

My queens, welcome to the second chapter of your journey—a journey of self-discovery, empowerment, and transformation. In this chapter, we will delve deep into the essence of what it means to embody grit and grace—the dynamic duo that will propel us forward on the path to becoming the best version of ourselves.

Grit, defined as courage, resolve, and strength of character, is the inner fire that fuels your journey. It is the unwavering determination to persevere in the face of adversity, push through obstacles with resilience and tenacity, and never waver in your pursuit of greatness. Grit is not just about sheer willpower or brute force; it is about harnessing the power of your innermost convictions and unleashing them upon the world with boldness and conviction.

But grit alone is not enough; it must be tempered with grace—the gentle yet powerful force that softens your edges, soothes your wounds, and infuses your journey with beauty and elegance. Grace is the embodiment of kindness, compassion, and humility—the qualities that will elevate you above the fray and enable you to survive life's challenges with poise and dignity.

In the sacred pages of Scripture, we find countless examples of women who embodied the perfect balance of grit and grace—women who faced insurmountable odds with unwavering resolve and never lost sight of the importance of extending grace to others.

Consider the story of Ruth, a Moabite woman who faced unimaginable loss and hardship yet remained steadfast in her commitment to her mother-in-law, Naomi. Ruth's grit was evident in her determination to work in the fields to provide for their needs despite the challenges she faced as a foreigner in a foreign land. And yet, it was her grace—the kindness and loyalty she showed to Naomi—that ultimately led to her redemption and restoration (Ruth 1-4, KJV).

Likewise, we find the story of Mary Magdalene, a woman who was once plagued by demons and darkness; she found redemption and healing in the presence of Jesus. Mary's grit was evident in her courage to follow Jesus to the cross, even when others had forsaken him. And yet, it was her grace—the love and devotion she showed to Jesus, even in the face of death—that earned her the honour of being the first witness to his resurrection (Matthew 27:55-61, KJV; John 20:11-18, KJV).

These biblical narratives serve as a powerful reminder of the transformative power of grit and grace—the dynamic duo that will empower you to rise above your circumstances and become the best version of yourselves. But how do you cultivate grit and grace in your own life? How do you harness the power of these virtues, enabling you to continue your journey through the challenges of life with courage, resilience, and grace?

It begins with a mindset shift—a conscious decision to embrace the inherent grit and grace that resides within each of you. It requires you to cultivate a spirit of perseverance, to confront your fears head-on, and to never waver in your pursuit of excellence. It also requires you to cultivate a spirit of grace—a willingness to extend kindness and compassion to yourself and others, even in the midst of adversity.

Cultivating grit and grace is not just about individual effort; it also requires community and support. You need sisters who will walk alongside you, encouraging, uplifting, and holding you accountable to your highest self. You need mentors who will impart wisdom and guidance, helping you to navigate the struggles and intricacies of life with grace and dignity.

Above all, you need faith—a deep and abiding trust in the power of the Most High to guide, strengthen, and sustain you on your journey. As the Apostle Paul reminds us, "I can do all things through Christ which strengtheneth me" (Philippians 4:13, KJV). With Christ as your anchor, you can face any challenge with grit and grace, knowing that you are never alone.

So, my lady, I implore you to embrace the power of grit and grace—the dynamic duo that will propel you forward on the path to becoming the best version of yourself. I pray that you will cultivate a spirit of perseverance, resilience, and tenacity tempered with kindness, compassion, and humility, and ultimately walk boldly and confidently into the future, knowing that with grit and grace, all things are possible.

CHAPTER 3

EMBRACING INNER BEAUTY

W omen of God and grace, as you journey deeper into the heart of your quest to become the best versions of yourselves, I need you to pause a moment to reflect on a truth that transcends the superficialities of external appearance. It is a truth that speaks to the essence of who you are—the truth that true beauty emanates from within.

In a world that often places undue emphasis on outward appearances, it can be easy to fall into the trap of equating beauty with physical attractiveness alone. All of us are continually bombarded daily with images of airbrushed perfection, leading us to believe that beauty is defined by flawless skin, slender figures, and symmetrical features. But as Bishop T. D. Jakes often reminds us, "Beauty is not defined by the size of your waist or the color of your skin. True beauty radiates from the depths of your soul."

In the Holy Bible, we find echoes of this truth, whispered through the ages to women of faith who understood that true beauty lies in the character of the heart. In the book of Proverbs, we read, "Favour is deceitful, and beauty is vain: but a woman that feareth the Lord, she shall be praised" (Proverbs 31:30, KJV). These words remind us that external beauty is fleeting and transient, but inner beauty—the beauty of a heart surrendered to the Most High—is everlasting and eternal.

But what does it mean to cultivate inner beauty? It begins with a heart transformed by love—a love that flows from the divine source of all creation and permeates every fiber of your being. It is a love that transcends boundaries and barriers, embracing all people as beloved children of the Most High.

Inner beauty is also reflected in the qualities of kindness, compassion, and humility. It is seen in acts of selflessness and service, in reaching out to those in need with hands of grace and hearts of compassion. It is found in the quiet moments of listening, comforting, and encouraging others, lifting their spirits and igniting the flame of hope within their souls.

In the Gospel of Matthew, Jesus teaches us, "Blessed are the pure in heart: for they shall see God" (Matthew 5:8, KJV). This verse speaks to the transformative power of purity of heart—a purity that is born out of a deep and abiding relationship with the Most High. It is a purity that reflects the beauty of holiness, shining forth like a beacon of light in a world darkened by sin and despair.

Precious ladies, as you strive to become the best versions of yourselves, always keep the reality in mind that true beauty is not found in the mirror on the wall but in the mirror of our souls. Continue to cultivate inner beauty—a beauty that radiates from the depths of your being and illuminates the world around you with the light of love, kindness, and compassion.

Cultivating inner beauty is not always easy; it requires effort, intentionality, and a willingness to confront the shadows that may attempt to lurk within your heart. It requires you to confront your fears, insecurities, and doubts and to surrender them to God in prayer and supplication. It requires you to cultivate a spirit of gratitude and thanksgiving, recognizing the blessings that abound in your lives and sharing them with others.

True beauty has never been found in the absence of flaws but rather in the splendor of grace. So, now is the perfect time to begin embracing your imperfections as sacred gifts, for they are the very things that make you unique and beautiful in the eyes of the Lord.

Continue striving to become women of inner beauty— women whose hearts are adorned with the jewels of love, kindness, and compassion. And ultimately allowing you to shine forth as brilliant lights in a world desperately in need of the transformative power of true beauty.

For true beauty begins within.

CHAPTER 4

SELF-DENIAL, SELF-DISCIPLINE, & SELF-CARE

My dear queens, as you continue this journey toward becoming the best versions of yourself, it is essential that you confront three crucial components of personal growth: self-denial, self-discipline, and self-care. These pillars are not merely suggestions for a balanced life; they are foundational principles that empower you to live with purpose, passion, and integrity.

Self-denial is the practice of sacrificing your own desires and preferences for the greater good—a concept often misunderstood in a culture that glorifies instant gratification and self-indulgence. Yet, as followers of the Most High, we are called to emulate the example of our Saviour, who "Made himself of no reputation, and took upon him the form of a servant" (Philippians 2:7, KJV). In denying ourselves, we align our hearts with the will of the Most High, surrendering our selfish ambitions and desires in exchange for a higher calling.

But self-denial alone is not enough; it must be coupled with self-discipline—the ability to regulate and control your thoughts, emotions, and actions in pursuit of your goals and aspirations. As the Apostle Paul writes, "I keep under my body, and bring it into subjection: lest that by any means, when I have preached to others, I myself should be a castaway" (1 Corinthians 9:27, KJV). Self-discipline requires you to exercise restraint and moderation in all areas of your lives, resisting the temptations of the flesh and staying focused on your journey towards self-improvement and personal growth.

Self-denial and self-discipline must also be balanced with self-care—the intentional practice of nurturing and nourishing your physical, emotional, and spiritual well-being. As the psalmist writes, "I will praise thee; for I am fearfully and wonderfully made" (Psalm 139:14, KJV). You are fearfully and wonderfully made by the Most High, and it is your sacred duty to honor and respect the temple of our bodies, minds, and spirits.

Self-care encompasses a wide range of practices, from nourishing your body with nutritious foods and regular exercise to nurturing your soul through prayer, meditation, and reflection. It requires you to set boundaries and prioritize your needs, recognizing that it is virtually insane to even believe that you could pour from an empty cup. It also involves surrounding yourself with positive influences and supportive relationships that uplift and inspire you on your journey.

But perhaps the most profound form of self-care is the practice of self-compassion—the ability to extend grace and forgiveness to ourselves in moments of weakness or failure. As the Apostle John writes, "If our heart condemn us not, then have we confidence toward God" (1 John 3:21, KJV). You must focus on treating yourself with the same kindness and compassion that you would offer to a beloved friend. Do you not think it is time for you to open the door to healing and transformation in your life?

Mighty woman, as you proceed through the pains and pressures of self-denial, self-discipline, and self-care, I need you to remember that you do not walk this journey alone. The Most High is ever-present, guiding you, strengthening you, and empowering you to become the best version of yourself. Lean on His wisdom and His grace, trusting that He will lead you to that path of righteousness and fulfillment.

Do not be afraid to lean on one another, for you are so much stronger together than you could ever be alone. Support and encourage one another as you strive to live lives of purpose, passion, and integrity. And please never lose sight of the beauty and the potential that resides within each and every one of you.

For in the practice of self-denial, self-discipline, and self-care, that is where you will discover the true essence of who you are—fearfully and wonderfully made by the Most High, destined for greatness, and empowered to shine forth as the silver lining in a grey world in need of hope and inspiration, in a world that needs you.

So, my lady, lovingly embrace these sacred principles with open hearts and willing spirits, knowing that in doing so, you will forever honor the divine spark that resides within you and illuminate your path to a brighter, more fulfilling future.

CHAPTER 5

UNLEASHING THE POWER OF VISION: SEEING THE UNSEEN

My dear queen, within each of you lies the power to envision a future that transcends your current circumstances—a future filled with purpose, passion, and limitless potential. Yet, far too often, you allow the distractions and pressures of daily life to cloud your vision, leaving you feeling adrift and directionless. But fear not, for within the depths of your soul resides a divine spark—a spark that, when ignited, has the power to illuminate the path to your greatest dreams and aspirations.

Vision is more than just a fanciful idea or fleeting thought; it is a powerful force that shapes your reality and propels you towards your destiny. As the Apostle Paul writes, "Where there is no vision, the people perish" (Proverbs 29:18, KJV). Without a clear vision to guide you, you are like ships adrift at sea, tossed to and fro by the winds of circumstance and uncertainty. But with vision, you move to the bottom of the ship, and you become captains of your fate, charting a course towards the fulfillment of your deepest desires and aspirations.

But what exactly is vision, and how do you unleash its power in your life? Vision is more than just seeing with your physical eyes; it is perceiving with the eyes of faith—the ability to see beyond the present moment and envision a future that aligns with the purpose and plan of the Most High. It is tapping into the crevices of the creativity and imagination that reside within each of you, daring to dream big and pursue your goals with unwavering determination and resolve.

In the book of Jeremiah, the Most High declares, "For I know the thoughts that I think toward you, saith the Lord, thoughts of peace, and not of evil, to give you an expected end" (Jeremiah 29:11, KJV). These words remind us all that God has a plan and a purpose for everyone—a plan filled with hope and promise, waiting to be revealed as you align your vision with His divine will.

But unleashing the power of vision requires more than just wishful thinking or idle dreaming; it requires action and intentionality. It requires you to cultivate a spirit of courage and boldness, stepping out of your comfort zone and embracing the unknown with confidence and faith. It also requires you to surround yourself with supportive and like-minded individuals who will encourage and uplift you on your journey.

In the Gospel of Mark, Jesus tells his disciples, "Therefore I say unto you, What things soever ye desire, when ye pray, believe that ye receive them, and ye shall have them" (Mark 11:24, KJV). These words are reminders of the power of faith—the power to manifest your vision into reality through the power of prayer and belief. When you align your hearts and minds with the vision that the Most High has placed within you, miracles begin to unfold, doors begin to open, and the impossible becomes possible.

However, perhaps the most important aspect of unleashing the power of vision is learning to trust in the timing and the process. Vision does not always unfold according to your timetable or in the manner that we expect, but it is always unfolding according to the perfect plan of the Most High. As the prophet Habakkuk writes, "For the vision is yet for an appointed time, but at the end, it shall speak, and not lie: though it tarry, wait for it; because it will surely come, it will not tarry" (Habakkuk 2:3, KJV).

So, my lady, I dare you to embrace the power of vision with open hearts and willing spirits, knowing that within you lies the power to create the life of your dreams. It is so important that you dream big, envision a future filled with purpose and passion, and pursue your goals with unwavering determination and resolve. And certainly trust in the divine timing and the perfect plan of the Most High, knowing that He who has begun a good work in us will bring it to completion.

For when you finally unleash the power of vision in your life, you will be empowered to tap into the infinite potential that lies within you, transforming your dreams into reality and your aspirations into achievements.

So, cast off the shackles of doubt and fear and embrace the vision that the good Lord has placed within you, for in the words of the poet, "The only thing worse than being blind is having sight but no vision."

CHAPTER 6

My Focus Is Stronger Than My Fear

My beloved sisters, in the pursuit of becoming the best versions of yourselves, we inevitably encounter moments of fear and uncertainty. It is a natural part of the human experience—a reminder of our vulnerability and our capacity for growth. Yet, despite the presence of fear, we are blessed to possess a power within us that is stronger, more resilient, and more enduring: our focus.

Focus is the brightly shining lamp that guides you through the storm, the North Star that illuminates your path when all else seems dark and uncertain. It is the unwavering commitment to your goals and aspirations, the laser-like precision that cuts through the noise and distractions of life, and the steadfast determination to press forward in the face of adversity.

In the Scripture, you will find countless examples of men and women who faced their fears with unwavering focus and determination. In the book of Joshua, the Most High commands Joshua, saying, "Be strong and of a good courage; be not afraid, neither be thou dismayed: for the Lord thy God is with thee whithersoever thou goest" (Joshua 1:9, KJV). Despite the daunting task set before him, Joshua remained focused on the promise of the Most High, leading the Israelites into the land of Canaan with unwavering resolve.

Likewise, we find in the story of Esther, a young woman who faced the fear of rejection and persecution as she stood before the king to plead for the lives of her people. Yet, in the face of danger, Esther remained focused on her mission, declaring, "If I perish, I perish" (Esther 4:16, KJV). Her focus on the greater good propelled her forward with courage and conviction, ultimately leading to the salvation of her people.

These biblical narratives serve as a powerful reminder of the transformative power of focus—the power to overcome fear and uncertainty and achieve your greatest aspirations. But how do you cultivate and maintain this unwavering focus in the midst of life's challenges?

It begins with clarity of purpose—a deep understanding of your goals, values, and aspirations. When you become crystal clear about what you want to achieve and why it matters to you, your focus becomes like a laser beam, cutting through the distractions and obstacles that stand in your way.

However, focus also requires discipline—a commitment to prioritize your time, energy, and resources in alignment with your goals. As the Apostle Paul writes, "I press toward the mark for the prize of the high calling of God in Christ Jesus"

(Philippians 3:14, KJV). Like a runner in a race, you must fix your eyes on the prize and press forward with perseverance and determination, refusing to be deterred by the challenges that lie ahead.

And perhaps most importantly, focus requires faith—a deep and abiding trust in the power of the Most High to guide you, strengthen you, and sustain you on your journey. As the psalmist writes, "I will lift up mine eyes unto the hills, from whence cometh my help. My help cometh from the Lord, which made heaven and earth" (Psalm 121:1-2, KJV). When you place your trust in the Most High, your focus becomes an anchor in the midst of the storm, grounding you in His peace and His presence.

So, my queens, embrace the power of focus with open hearts and willing spirits, knowing that within lies the strength to overcome any fear or obstacle that stands in your way. Let us fix our eyes on the prize, press forward with determination, and trust in the guiding hand of the Most High to lead us to victory.

When your focus is stronger than your fear, there is no limit to what you can achieve. So, stand firm in your resolve, knowing that with the Most High by your side, you are completely unstoppable.

CHAPTER 7

I AM A WARRIOR. I AM A WORSHIPPER. I AM A WOMAN

My dear queens, as you continue on your journey towards self-discovery and empowerment, continue to diligently embrace the multifaceted roles that define you as women of strength, resilience, and grace. For within each of you resides the heart of a warrior, the spirit of a worshipper, and the essence of womanhood—a powerful combination that empowers you to overcome every obstacle and achieve your greatest aspirations.

First and foremost, let us explore the role of the warrior—a fierce and courageous guardian of truth, justice, and righteousness. In the Scripture, we find countless examples of women who embodied the spirit of the warrior, fearlessly confronting adversity and standing firm in their convictions. From Deborah, the prophetess and judge who led the Israelites to victory in battle, to Jael, who boldly struck down the enemy with a tent peg, these women exemplify the strength and resilience of the warrior spirit.

But what does it mean to be a warrior in the modern world? It means standing up for what is right, even when it is difficult or unpopular. It means advocating for justice and equality, fighting against oppression and injustice in all its forms. It means facing your fears head-on, confronting your doubts and insecurities, and emerging stronger and more determined than ever before.

Yet, alongside the spirit of the warrior, we must also embrace the role of the worshipper—a humble and devoted servant of the Most High whose heart is attuned to the rhythms of praise and adoration. In the book of Psalms, we read, "Give unto the Lord the glory due unto his name; worship the Lord in the beauty of holiness" (Psalm 29:2, KJV). As worshippers, we have a very specific calling and role. We are called to lift those anointed voices in praise and thanksgiving, acknowledging the greatness of the Most High and surrendering ourselves to His will.

But worship is more than just a series of rituals or religious observances; it is a way of life—a posture of humility and reverence that permeates every aspect of your being. It is found in the quiet moments of prayer and meditation, as well as in the joyful celebrations of community and fellowship. It is a reminder that as dark and miserable as it may be, you are not alone, but you are held in the loving embrace of the Most High, who delights in your worship and draws near to you in moments of praise and adoration.

And finally, let us celebrate the essence of womanhood—a

beautiful rainbow of strength, compassion, and grace that distinguishes you as a daughter of the Most High. In the book of Proverbs, we read, "Who can find a virtuous woman? For her price is far above rubies" (Proverbs 31:10, KJV). Women, you are fearfully and wonderfully made, endowed with unique gifts and talents that enable you to enrich the world around you.

But being a woman is not without its challenges. You face societal expectations and cultural stereotypes that seek to diminish your worth and limit your potential. Yet, in the face of adversity, you rise with resilience and determination, embracing your identities with pride and purpose.

So, my lady, do indeed embrace the roles of warrior, worshipper, and woman with open hearts and willing spirits, knowing that within you lies the power to overcome every obstacle and achieve your greatest aspirations. Continue to stand firm in your convictions, lift your voices in praise and adoration, and celebrate the beauty and strength of womanhood in all its glory.

For you are warriors, fearlessly confronting adversity and injustice; you are worshippers, lifting your voices in praise and thanksgiving; and above all, you are women, fearfully and wonderfully made by the Most High, destined for greatness and empowered to shine forth as beams of light in a world in need of hope and inspiration.

CHAPTER 8

INSTINCTS OF A MOTHER

My dear queens, as you journey through the complications of life, there exists within each of you a divine source of strength, wisdom, and love—the instincts of a mother. These instincts are not merely biological; they are a sacred gift from the Most High, bestowed upon women as stewards of life and nurturers of the soul.

In the scriptures, we find countless examples of women who embodied the instincts of a mother—women who demonstrated unwavering love, compassion, and sacrifice for their children and their communities. From the selfless devotion of Mary, the mother of Jesus, to the fierce protection of Jochebed, who risked her own life to save her son Moses from Pharaoh's decree, these women exemplify the timeless qualities of maternal instinct.

But what exactly are the instincts of a mother, and how do they manifest in your daily lives? At its core, the instinct of a mother is a deep and abiding love—a love that transcends boundaries and defies logic, a love that is fierce yet tender, unconditional yet unwavering. It is a love that compels us all to put the needs of others before our own, to sacrifice and serve with a selflessness that knows no bounds.

But maternal instinct is not just about love; it is also about intuition—the innate ability to sense the needs and emotions of your children and respond with empathy and compassion. It is the gentle whisper that will guide you in moments of uncertainty, the quiet knowing that assures you that you are indeed on the right path. It is a gift from the Most High, bestowed upon women as divine caretakers and guardians of life.

And perhaps most importantly, the instincts of a mother are rooted in faith—a deep and abiding trust in the providence and protection of the Most High. In the book of Isaiah, we read, "Can a woman forget her sucking child, that she should not have compassion on the son of her womb? Yea, they may forget, yet will I not forget thee" (Isaiah 49:15, KJV). These words remind us that the love of the Most High surpasses even the deepest bonds of maternal affection and that He is ever-present, guiding and sustaining us on your journey.

As you embrace the instincts of a mother, know that you are not alone. The Most High has entrusted you with a sacred responsibility—to nurture and protect the lives entrusted to your care, to shape and mold the hearts and minds of the next generation. And He has equipped you with everything you need to fulfill this calling—the love, the intuition, and the faith to overcome every obstacle and challenge that may come your way.

But beyond the traditional roles of motherhood, the instincts of a mother extend far beyond biological ties. They encompass the nurturing spirit that women bring to all aspects of life—their families, their communities, and the world at large. Women possess a unique ability to nurture and empower others, to offer comfort and support in times of need, and to inspire and uplift with their strength and resilience.

In a world that often diminishes the contributions of women, it is essential to recognize and celebrate the instincts of a mother—their boundless capacity for love, their intuitive wisdom, and their unwavering faith. These instincts are not just a part of who we are; they are the very essence of your being, woven into the fabric of your souls by the hand of the Most High.

So, my dear sisters, embrace the instincts of a mother with open arms and willing hearts, knowing that within you lies the power to nurture and inspire, to heal and uplift, to love and to cherish, for you are fearfully and wonderfully made, endowed with the divine essence of motherhood—a sacred gift from the Most High, to be cherished and celebrated for all eternity.

CHAPTER 9

BROKEN RELATIONSHIPS, HEALING HANDS

M y dear queens, there is a truth that rests at the edge of your lives. A reality that we sometimes attempt to avoid. We all will inevitably encounter moments of brokenness—fractured relationships that leave us feeling wounded, scarred, and alone. Yet, even in the midst of your pain and heartache, there exists a profound opportunity for healing and restoration—a chance to mend the broken pieces of your lives and emerge stronger, wiser, and more resilient than before.

In the Holy Bible, we find a God who is intimately acquainted with the pain of broken relationships—a God who, in His infinite love and mercy, offers healing and restoration to all who come to Him with open hearts and willing spirits. In the book of Psalms, we read, "The Lord is nigh unto them that are of a broken heart; and saveth such as be of a contrite spirit" (Psalm

34:18, KJV). These words remind us that we are not alone in our pain but that the Most High is ever-present, ready to wrap you in His loving embrace and heal your deepest wounds.

But how does one journey the tumultuous waters of broken relationships with grace and dignity? How do you find healing and restoration in the midst of your pain and heartache? It begins with a willingness to confront your pain—to acknowledge the hurt and disappointment that you feel and to bring your brokenness before the Most High in prayer and supplication. As the Apostle Peter writes, "Casting all your care upon him; for he careth for you" (1 Peter 5:7, KJV). When you surrender your pain and brokenness to the Most High, you open the door to healing and restoration in your lives.

But healing from broken relationships also requires forgiveness—a conscious decision to release the grip of bitterness and resentment and extend grace and compassion to those who have wronged you. In the Gospel of Matthew, Jesus teaches us to pray, "Forgive us our debts, as we forgive our debtors" (Matthew 6:12, KJV). Forgiveness is not just a gift that we extend to others; it is a gift that we give to ourselves, freeing us from the chains of unforgiveness and allowing us to move forward with joy and peace in our hearts.

Yet, forgiveness does not always come easily. It requires courage and humility to lay down your pride and ego, to let go of the need for vengeance and retribution, and to embrace the transformative power of love and grace. But when we choose to forgive, we open the door to healing and reconciliation, paving the way for the restoration of broken relationships and the renewal of hope and trust.

And finally, healing from broken relationships requires a commitment to personal growth and self-discovery—a willingness to reflect on the lessons learned from your experiences and to embrace the opportunity for growth and transformation. In the book of Romans, the Apostle Paul writes, "And we know that all things work together for good to them that love God, to them who are the called according to his purpose" (Romans 8:28, KJV). Even in the midst of your pain and brokenness, the Most High can use your experiences to shape and mold you into the woman He has called you to be.

As you journey through the process of healing from broken relationships, I pray that you remember that you are not defined by your past hurts or failures but by the strength and resilience with which you rise from them. It is time to embrace the opportunity to cultivate compassion and empathy for yourself and others, recognizing that you are all imperfect beings in need of grace and understanding.

When navigating the hurts, damages, and broken pieces of broken relationships, know that the Most High is with you every step of the way, guiding and comforting you with His unfailing love and grace. He sees your pain, He hears your cries, and He stands ready to heal your brokenness and restore your hope.

So, take heart and hold fast to the promise of healing

and restoration. For in the hands of the Most High, even the deepest wounds can be healed, and the broken pieces of your lives can be transformed into a beautiful mosaic of redemption and grace. Trust in His timing, His wisdom, and His unfailing love, knowing that He who began a good work in you will carry it on to completion until the day of Christ Jesus (Philippians 1:6, KJV).

May you find comfort and strength in His presence, and may His healing hands guide you on the journey to wholeness and restoration. Broken relationships may leave scars, but they also provide an opportunity for growth, healing, and renewal. And in the end, it is through your brokenness that you will find your greatest strength and your deepest connection to the Most High.

CHAPTER 10

MOVING FROM PUNISHED TO PURPOSED

My dear queens, life is filled with moments of trial and tribulation—times when you feel as though you are being punished for your mistakes, your shortcomings, and your failures. Yet, even in the midst of your darkest moments, there exists a divine purpose—a higher calling that begs for you to rise above your circumstances and embrace the fullness of who you are meant to be.

As we scour through the Scripture, we find countless examples of individuals who moved from a place of punishment to a place of purpose—men and women who endured hardship and adversity, only to emerge stronger, wiser, and more determined than ever before. In the book of Genesis, we read the story of Joseph, who was betrayed by his brothers, sold into slavery, and unjustly imprisoned. Yet, through it all, Joseph remained steadfast in his faith, trusting in the plan and the purpose of the Most High. In the end, he rose to become a mighty ruler in Egypt, saving his family and his people from famine and destruction.

But how does one move from a place of feeling punished to a place of embracing one's divine purpose? It begins with a shift in perspective—a willingness to see your trials and tribulations not as punishments but as opportunities for growth and transformation. In the book of Romans, the Apostle Paul writes, "And we know that all things work together for good to them that love God, to them who are the called according to his purpose" (Romans 8:28, KJV). Even in your darkest moments, the Most High is at work, weaving together the threads of your lives into a beautiful display of redemption and grace.

But embracing your divine purpose also requires faith—a deep and abiding trust in the wisdom and the providence of the Most High. In the book of Jeremiah, the Most High declares, "For I know the thoughts that I think toward you, saith the Lord, thoughts of peace, and not of evil, to give you an expected end" (Jeremiah 29:11, KJV). Though we may not always understand His ways, we can trust that He has a plan and a purpose for our lives—a plan filled with hope and promise, waiting to be revealed in His perfect timing.

Yet, finding your divine purpose also requires action—a willingness to step out in faith and pursue your dreams and aspirations with courage and determination. In the Gospel of Matthew, Jesus tells His disciples, "Ye are the light of the world. A city that is set on a hill cannot be hidden" (Matthew 5:14, KJV). Each of us has been endowed with unique gifts and talents placed within us by the Most High for a specific purpose. It is up to us to uncover those gifts, cultivate them, and use them to make a positive impact on the world around us.

Finally, moving from a place of feeling punished to a place of embracing your divine purpose requires forgiveness—a willingness to forgive ourselves for past mistakes and failures and to extend grace and compassion to others who may have wronged us. In the Gospel of Luke, Jesus says, "Forgive, and ye shall be forgiven" (Luke 6:37, KJV). When you release the burdens of unforgiveness and resentment, you create space in your hearts for healing and transformation, allowing yourself to fully embrace the purpose and the calling that the Most High has placed within yourself.

So, as you forge ahead and through the challenges and trials of life, remember that you are not defined by your mistakes or your failures. You are a beloved child of the Most High, endowed with purpose and potential beyond measure. Trust in His plan, His timing, and His unfailing love, knowing that He who began a good work in you will carry it on to completion until the day of Christ Jesus (Philippians 1:6, KJV).

May you move from a place of feeling punished to a place of embracing your divine purpose, shining forth as a beacon of light and hope in a world in need of your unique gifts and talents. For in the end, it is through your trials and tribulations that you will certainly discover the fullness of who you are meant to be, and it is through your brokenness that you will fully distinguish your greatest strength and your deepest connection to the Most High.

CHAPTER 11

LOVE'S LEGACY, COMPLIMENTS OF YOU

M y dear queens, within each of you lies a boundless reservoir of love—a love that has the power to transform lives, mend broken hearts, and leave an indelible mark on the world. This love is not merely a fleeting emotion or a passing feeling; it is a sacred gift from the Most High, bestowed upon you as stewards of His grace and ambassadors of His love.

In the pages of the Bible, we find the greatest expression of love in the person of Jesus Christ. In the Gospel of John, we read, "For God so loved the world, that he gave his only begotten Son, that whosoever believeth in him should not perish, but have everlasting life" (John 3:16, KJV). This profound act of sacrificial love serves as the ultimate example for us all—a reminder of the power and the potency of love to overcome even the greatest obstacles and challenges.

But what does it mean to leave a legacy of love? It means living your lives with intentionality and purpose, seeking opportunities to sow seeds of kindness, compassion, and grace in the lives of those around you. It means embracing the call to love one another as the Most High has loved us, extending mercy and forgiveness to all who cross our paths.

Yet, leaving a legacy of love also requires you to embrace the fullness of who you are—to recognize and celebrate the unique gifts and talents that the Most High has bestowed upon you and to use them for the betterment of humanity. In the book of Ephesians, the Apostle Paul writes, "For we are his workmanship, created in Christ Jesus unto good works, which God hath before ordained that we should walk in them" (Ephesians 2:10, KJV). Each of us has been created with a divine purpose and a unique calling, and it is through the expression of your gifts and talents that you will leave a lasting legacy of love in the world.

But perhaps most importantly, leaving a legacy of love requires us to cultivate a heart of gratitude—a deep and abiding appreciation for the blessings and opportunities that the Most High has bestowed upon us. In the book of Psalms, we read, "O give thanks unto the Lord; for he is good: for his mercy endureth forever" (Psalm 136:1, KJV). When approaching life with a spirit of gratitude and thanksgiving, your heart becomes an overflowing fountain of love, pouring out blessings upon all who come into your presence.

So, as you journey through life, may you be ever mindful of the legacy of love that you are leaving behind. May you embrace the call to love one another with sincerity and compassion, and may you use your gifts and talents to make a positive impact in the lives of those around you. For in the end, it is not the wealth or the fame that we leave behind that matters most, but the love that we have shared and the lives that we have touched along the way.

May you be blessed with the courage to love boldly, the strength to forgive freely, and the grace to leave a legacy of love that will endure for generations to come. For love is the greatest legacy of all—a precious gift from the Most High, compliments of you.

CHAPTER 12

Sometimes Silent, But Always Spiritual

My dear queens, there is a profound elegance in the quiet strength of a woman—a strength that speaks volumes without uttering a single word, a strength that emanates from the depths of her soul and radiates with a grace that is both captivating and awe-inspiring. In a world that often celebrates the loudest voices and the boldest actions, it is the quiet, steadfast presence of a queen that leaves an indelible mark on the hearts and minds of those around her.

In the sacred scriptures, we find numerous examples of women who embodied this quiet strength and spiritual poise—women like Ruth, whose loyalty and devotion to her mother-in-law Naomi led her to glean in the fields of Boaz, ultimately securing a future for herself and Naomi. Ruth's quiet determination and unwavering faith in the Most High set her apart, earning her a place of honor in the lineage of King David and, ultimately, the Messiah Himself.

But what does it mean to be sometimes silent yet always spiritual? It means possessing a depth of character and inner fortitude that transcends the need for constant affirmation or recognition. It means being rooted in a faith that sustains you through life's trials and tribulations, guiding your steps with wisdom and grace.

The storms of life do not easily rattle queens who embody this balance of quiet strength and spiritual depth. They are like the proverbial tree planted by the rivers of water, whose leaf does not wither and who bears fruit in due season (Psalm 1:3, KJV). They draw their strength from the deep, righteous reservoirs of the Most High's love and find refuge in His presence, even in the midst of life's fiercest battles.

Yet, sometimes being silent but always spiritual does not mean being passive or indifferent. On the contrary, it means being actively engaged in the work of the Most High, whether it be in the home, workplace, or community. It means leading by example, demonstrating compassion, integrity, and wisdom in all that you do.

In the book of Proverbs, we read, "She openeth her mouth with wisdom; and in her tongue is the law of kindness" (Proverbs 31:26, KJV). This verse speaks to the power of a woman's words when spoken with intentionality and grace. Queens who are sometimes silent but always spiritual understand the impact of their words and use them to uplift and inspire those around them.

In the book of Psalms, we find solace and wisdom: "Be still, and know that I am God" (Psalm 46:10, KJV). These words resonate with the essence of queens who are sometimes silent yet always spiritual. They understand the power of silence—to quiet the mind, to calm the spirit, and to open oneself to the gentle whisperings of the divine.

The storms of life do not easily rattle queens who possess this quiet strength. They stand firm in their convictions, anchored by a deep and abiding faith that sustains them through every trial and tribulation. Theirs is a resilience born of trust in the Most High, a trust that allows them to weather life's challenges with grace and poise.

But being silent sometimes does not mean being passive or indifferent. On the contrary, it is a deliberate choice—a conscious decision to listen more than they speak, to observe more than they react. In the book of Proverbs, we are reminded: "Even a fool, when he holdeth his peace, is counted wise: and he that shutteth his lips is esteemed a man of understanding" (Proverbs 17:28, KJV). These queens understand the power of restraint, knowing that their words carry weight and impact.

Their silence is not a sign of weakness but of inner strength—a strength that comes from knowing when to speak and when to listen, when to act and when to wait patiently. They possess a wisdom that transcends words, a wisdom that speaks volumes even in the void and complete absence of sound.

As you strive to embody the attributes and poise of queens who are sometimes silent yet always spiritual, may you find strength and solace in the knowledge that you are never alone. The Most High walks beside you, guiding your steps and illuminating your path with His divine light.

May you draw upon the wellspring of spiritual wisdom and grace that resides within you, finding refuge in the quiet moments of prayer and meditation, and may you walk with confidence and assurance, knowing that you are a queen—a woman of strength, dignity, and grace—whose quiet presence speaks volumes in a world in need of hope and inspiration.

I pray that you continue to cultivate inner peace and quiet strength, trusting in the wisdom and guidance of the Most High. And that you may walk with grace and dignity, knowing that you are daughters of the Most High, endowed with a beauty and strength that can never be diminished.

Made in the USA
Middletown, DE
28 June 2024